SPIKE and CHAIN
Japanese Fighting Arts

SPIKE
and
CHAIN
Japanese Fighting Arts

by Charles V. Gruzanski

CHARLES E. TUTTLE CO.: PUBLISHERS
Rutland, Vermont & Tokyo, Japan

Representatives
Continental Europe: BOXERBOOKS, INC., *Zurich*
British Isles: PRENTICE-HALL INTERNATIONAL, INC., *London*
Australasia: PAUL FLESCH & CO., PTY. LTD., *Melbourne*
Canada: M. G. HURTIG LTD., *Edmonton*

Published by the Charles E. Tuttle Company, Inc.
of Rutland, Vermont & Tokyo, Japan
with editorial offices at Suido 1-chome, 2-6
Bunkyo-ku, Tokyo, Japan

Copyright in Japan, 1968 by Charles E. Tuttle Co., Inc.

Library of Congress Catalog Card No. 68-15019

Standard Book No. 8048 0540-7

First edition, 1968
Second printing, 1970

PRINTED IN JAPAN

Table of Contents

LIST OF ILLUSTRATIONS 11

ACKNOWLEDGMENTS 17

PREFACE 19

INTRODUCTION 21

THE SAMURAI CREED 23

PART I MASAKI-RYU

History of the *Manrikigusari* and *Masaki-ryu* 27
   The Beginning
   Development of the Art
   Other Schools of the *Manrikigusari*

Special Characteristics of the *Manrikigusari* 31
   General Features
   Advantages to Using the *Manrikigusari*
   Practice
   Unique Features

Techniques for Using the *Manrikigusari* 35
   Proper Grip
   Manipulation
   Kamae (Preparatory Positions)
      Goho-no-kamae 36 ● *Issei-no-kamae* 39
      ● *Tenchi-no-kamae* 40 ● *Shumoku-no-kamae* 41 ● *Ippu-no-kamae* 42

Iai Techniques

    Kasumi (hazing 43 ● *Kakoiuchi* (vertical downward strike including the vertical "figure 8") 47 ● *Sukuichi* (scooping strike in an upward direction to include the horizontal "figure 8") 49 ● *Kobushigarami-nage katame* (fist winding and throwing technique) 51 ● *Udegatame-nage katame* (forearm lock and throwing technique) 54 ● *Jodan-uke* (upper block) 56 ● *Uchiotoshi* (striking drop) 58 ● *Shohatsu* (horizontal strike) 59 ● *Ukenagashi* (flowing block) 61 ● *Makiotoshi* (winding drop) 63 ● *Yukichigai* (draw and strike) 64 ● *Nageuchi* (throwing strike), *ichidan* and *nidan* 66

Tachiai Techniques

    Yokonagare (checking technique) 68 ● *Samidare-no-uchi* (body shifting, horizontal striking, and kick) 68 ● *Kagero-no-uchi* (body shifting, vertical upward striking, and kick) 69 ● *Yadome* (arrow stop or shield technique) 69

Henka (variations)

    Kobushi kujiki (fist crushing) 70 ● *Suneori* (shin striking) 70

Other Variations

    Defense against one hand chain seizure 71 ● Defense against two hand chain seizure 72 ● Defense against kicking 74

Kyusho (vital points of the human body) 77

How to Make a *Manrikigusari* 85

    The Chain

    The Weights

PART II SHURIKEN-JUTSU

History of *Shuriken-jutsu* 91

The Transition 92

Various Types of *Shuriken* 92

Proper Method of Holding the *Shuriken* 93

The Secrets of *Shuriken-jutsu* 94

Practice 96

Half-turn Method 97

Target Selection 97

Safety Precautions 98

Throwing and Distance 98

How to Make Your Own *Shuriken* 100

Shaken (Cross-shaped *Shuriken*) 101

BIBLIOGRAPHY 103

List of Illustrations

1. The *manrikigusari* used against the samurai sword 26
2. Master Yumio Nawa 29
3. Examples of several authentic *manrikigusari* 33
4. Different types of *manrikigusari* 33
5. Initial grip of the *manrikigusari* 37
6. The proper complete grip of the *manrikigusari* 37
7. Grip for attacking the eyes 38
8. Method of attacking the temple 38
9. *Goho-no-kamae* (front view) 38
10. *Goho-no-kamae* (side view) 38
11. *Issei-no-kamae* (front view) 39
12. *Issei-no-kamae* (side view) 39
13. *Tenchi-no-kamae* (front view) 40
14. *Tenchi-no-kamae* (side view) 40
15. *Shumoku-no-kamae* (front view) 41
16. *Shumoku-no-kamae* (side view) 41
17. *Ippu-no-kamae* (front view) 42
18. *Ippu-no-kamae* (rear view) 42
19. *Goho-no-kamae* 44
20. *Issei-no-kamae* 44
21. *Kasumi* against approach from the right 45
22. *Kasumi* against approach from the left 45
23. *Kasumi* against approach from the rear 45
24. *Kakoiuchi* 46
25. *Tenchi-no-kamae* 46

26. *Shumoku-no-kamae* 46
27. *Ippu-no-kamae* 46
28. Striking position for *kakoiuchi* (front) 48
29. Striking position for *kakoiuchi* (side) 48
30. Vertical "figure 8" 48
31. *Issei-no-kamae* 49
32. *Shumoku-no-kamae* 50
33. *Ippu-no-kamae* 50
34. Horizontal "figure 8" 50
35. *Tenchi-no-kamae* 51
36. *Kobushigarami* (placing the chain in horizontal position under opponent's wrist) 52
37. Winding the chain around the wrist 52
38. Pulling the opponent to the ground 52
39. Striking the fallen opponent with *kakoiuchi* 52
40. Forearm lock 53
41. Kicking the tailbone with the knee 53
42. Placing the leg behind the opponent 53
43. Pushing the opponent to the ground 53
44. Striking the fallen opponent with *kakoiuchi* with the right hand 53
45. *Tenchi-no-kamae* 54
46. *Shumoku-no-kamae* 54
47. Locking the arm in *udegatame* 55
48. Striking the opponent's ribs with the left hand 55
49. Placing the leg behind the opponent 55
50. Throwing the opponent to the ground 55
51. Striking the opponent with *kakoiuchi* with the left hand 55
52. *Tenchi-no-kamae* 56
53. *Shumoku-no-kamae* 56
54. Defensive position for defense against overhead blow 57
55. Defending with *jodan-uke* 57

56. Striking the opponent's eyes 57
57. Avoiding the opponent's punch in *uchiotoshi* 58
58. Throwing the chain around the opponent's wrist 58
59. Pulling the opponent to the ground 58
60. *Tenchi-no-kamae* 59
61. *Shumoku-no-kamae* 60
62. Striking out with *shohatsu* 60
63. Striking the opponent with *shohatsu* 60
64. *Goho-no-kamae* 61
65. *Tenchi-no-kamae* 61
66. *Shumoku-no-kamae* 61
67. Holding the chain slack 62
68. Blocking diagonally with *ukenagashi* 62
69. Striking the opponent's eyes 62
70. *Goho-no-kamae* 63
71. *Tenchi-no-kamae* 63
72. *Shumoku-no-kamae* 63
73. Looping the chain around the opponent's neck in *makiotoshi* 63
74. Carrying the *manrikigusari* on the belt 64
75. Drawing the *manrikigusari* from the belt 64
76. Striking the opponent's chin with *sukuiuchi* 65
77. Striking the opponent across the back with doubled chain 65
78. *Goho-no-kamae* 66
79. *Issei-no-kamae* 66
80. *Nageuchi ichidan* 67
81. *Nageuchi nidan* 67
82. Throwing the chain around the fleeing opponent's ankle 67
83. *Yokonagare* 68
84. *Samidare-no-uchi* 68
85. *Kagero-no-uchi* 69
86. *Yadome* 69

87. *Kobushi kujiki* 70
88. *Suneori* 70
89. One hand chain seizure 71
90. Two hand chain seizure 72
91. Winding the chain around the opponent's wrists 72
92. Raising the opponent's arms 73
93. Inserting the left shoulder under the opponent's elbows 73
94. Pulling the opponent forward and lifting with the legs 73
95. Throwing the opponent over the shoulder and to the ground 73
96. Winding the chain around the opponent's ankle in defense of a kick 74
97. Countering the opponent's kick with a kick to the vital points 74
98. Catching the opponent's leg in defense of a kick 75
99. Raising the opponent's leg to throw him to the ground 75
100. Hooking the opponent's leg 75
101. Throwing the opponent by reaping his leg 75
102. *Kyusho*-vital points of the human body (front) 78
103. *Kyusho*-vital points of the human body (rear) 79
104. Specifications for making a *manrikigusari* 87
105. Samurai throwing the *shaken* 90
106. Various kinds of *shuriken* 93
107. Proper method of holding the *shuriken* (point up) 94
108. Proper method of holding the *shuriken* (point down) 94
109. Stance for throwing the *shuriken* at short distances 95
110. Stance for throwing the *shuriken* at longer distances 95
111. An outdoor target for throwing the *shuriken* 98

112. Length of some *shuriken* shown in inches 100
113. Various kinds of *shaken* 101
114. Method of attacking the eyes with the *shuriken* 102
115. Method of attacking the throat with the *shuriken* 102

Acknowledgments

To the following persons I extend my sincere appreciation for their contributions to the successful compilation of this work.

Mr. YUMIO NAWA and the Yuzankaku Publishing Company, Tokyo, for their kind permission to use excerpts and illustrations from the book, *Jutte Hojo-no Kenkyu* (The Arresting Rope Study).

Mr. RAY FALK, Globe Photos, Inc., and *Argosy Magazine* for their kind permission to use photographs from the article "Art of Invisibility" which appeared in the May 1961 issue of *Argosy*.

Mr. TOM JAWORSKI, for his fine photographs of the techniques that appear herein.

Mr. LUPE MEDINA, for his excellent sketch of the *manrikigusari*.

Reverend SOYU MATSUOKA, for his excellent translating.

Mrs. ROSE SZCZESNY, for undertaking the task of typing the manuscript.

Mr. HENRY E. SARABIA, for his assistance in demonstrating the techniques.

Preface

IN REVEALING the secrets of Masaki-Ryu and Shuriken-Jutsu, the author gives much needed information and instruction in two arts of self-defense—the *manrikigusari* and the *shuriken*—previously little known or understood in the West and valuable storehouses of knowledge in themselves.

But, most important of all is the author's appreciation of the spirit of Zen in the martial arts. This book could not be written without it. Because of his lengthy instruction by the masters in Japan in martial arts, and because of his receptive, open mind, he has long recognized the need for Zen in the defensive arts. Years of experience in both teaching and practicing the martial arts in the spirit and tempo of Zen have convinced him of its dire necessity.

This delicate balance between the mental, spiritual, and physical is maintained solely by the practice of Zen. It cannot be omitted from a book on martial arts. One should read *all* of this book. The author has made great efforts to make his study, practice, and presentation of the arts of self-defense true to their Oriental origin. Read this book and profit richly by it.

Rev. Soyu Matsuoka
Zen Buddhist Temple of Chicago

Introduction

THE JAPANESE arts of *Masaki-Ryu* and *Shuriken-Jutsu* are very old. Their practicality for use in self-defense situations will be left by the author to the intelligence and imagination of the reader.

For enthusiasts of the martial arts, this work should broaden your knowledge considerably. For those who wish to use the *manrikigusari* or *shuriken* for wrongdoing, a warning is issued that irresponsible use in injuring others or damaging property will result in physical and spiritual destruction. Even the broadest interpretation of the law will classify them as deadly or dangerous weapons.

Remember that the weapons and techniques illustrated in this book cannot injure anyone by themselves. It is the person behind them that really makes them dangerous.

The Samurai Creed

I have no parents; I make the heavens and the earth my parents.

I have no home; I make *saika tanden* (abdominal region) my home.

I have no divine power; I make honesty my divine power.

I have no means; I make docility my means.

I have no magic power; I make personality my magic power.

I have neither life nor death; I make *a um* (art of regulating one's breath) my life and death.

I have no body; I make stoicism my body.

I have no eyes; I make the flash of lightning my eyes.

I have no ears; I make sensibility my ears.

I have no limbs; I make promptitude my limbs.

I have no laws; I make self-protection my laws.

I have no strategy; I make *sakkatsu jizai* (free to kill and free to restore life) my strategy.

I have no designs; I make *kisan* (taking opportunity by the forelock) my designs.

I have no miracles; I make righteous laws my miracles.

I have no principles; I make *rinkiohen* (adaptability to all circumstances) my principles.

I have no tactics; I make *kyojitsu* (emptiness and fullness) my tactics.

I have no talent; I make *toi sokumyo* (ready wit) my talent.

I have no friends; I make my mind my friend.

I have no enemy; I make incautiousness my enemy.

I have no armor; I make *jin-gi* (benevolence and righteousness) my armor.

I have no castle; I make *fudoshin* (immovable mind) my castle.

I have no sword; I make *mushin* (absence of mind) my sword.

PART I
THE SECRETS OF
MASAKI-RYU

1. The *manrikigusari* used against the samurai sword

History of
the *Manrikigusari*
and *Masaki-ryu*

The Beginning

ACCORDING to the written records of *Masaki-ryu*, the founder of the *manrikigusari* and the person chiefly responsible for its development is Dannoshin Toshimitsu Masaki—one of the most famous and skillful swordsmen of his day.

While assigned as Head Sentry for the main gate of Edo (Tokyo) Castle, it was the responsibility of Masaki and his disciples to guard against the intrusion of bandits, hoodlums, or otherwise insane persons. It was at that time that Masaki became aware and gravely concerned that should an attempt be made to breach the gate, it would certainly result in the heavy flow of blood.

Masaki's convictions dictated that such bloody battles should not take place before such a famous and important gate. He felt that a sword should never be unsheathed at such a sacred place nor should it be soiled with blood, yet the castle gate must be defended at all costs. For some time to follow, Masaki gave considerable thought to what type of weapon would be most appropriate. For reasons known only to himself, he decided that the use of the chain in some form would be most suitable for defending not only against unarmed enemies, but those armed with sticks, swords, and other types of weapons. As a result he constructed many kinds of chain weapons with iron weights attached to them—this was the birth of the *manrikigusari*. (These events are alleged to have occurred about two hundred years ago.)

Development of the Art

Masaki then taught the techniques of the chain to his disciples and students of the sword, and founded the *Masaki-Ryu* (or Masaki School). Masaki named his weapon "*Manrikigusari*" (*manriki* meaning "10,000-power" and *gusari*, "chain") because he felt it contained the power and ingenuity of 10,000 persons.

In the time that followed, it was not long before the *manrikigusari* became famous throughout Japan. People came from all corners of Japan to secure the *manrikigusari* and to learn its techniques and secrets. Before Masaki presented the *manrikigusari* to anyone or before he taught its techniques, he always instructed the receiver that the *manrikigusari* was not meant for unnecessary fighting and that it should be used only for right. Should it be used for wrongdoing, Masaki warned that that person would destroy himself physically and spiritually. Upon presenting the *manrikigusari*, Masaki is said to have bowed and with a prayer sought to inject a good spirit in it before presenting it to a patron.

The art of *manrikigusari* was adopted at the Ogaki Samurai Headquarters (Ogaki City, Gifu Prefecture) soon after. At that time an ancestor of Yumio Nawa (author of *Jutte Hojo-No Kenkyu* cited in the *Acknowledgment*) was Superintendent and Administer of Justice for Samurai. The art then descended to him from his grandfather.

For many years the *manrikigusari* was taught in the Ogaki High School as a part of its regular curriculum just as judo, kendo, and other martial arts are taught in schools

2. Master Yumio Nawa

throughout Japan today. But, because of its misuse by some of the students at that time, the course was discontinued. Today at Ogaki Castle there are approximately 15 *manrikigusari* displayed with a complete history, which is all that remains of this dying and almost extinct art.

Other Schools of the *Manrikigusari*

From *Masaki-ryu* there grew many different *ryu* (or schools) of the chain throughout Japan. Today in Japan there is said to be only about 20 that remain. Some of these are: *Hoen-ryu*, *Toda-ryu*, *Shuchin-ryu*, *Kyoshin-Meichi-ryu*, *Shindo-ryu*, and *Hikida-ryu*. The basic difference in some of these *ryu* as compared to *Masaki-ryu* is the length of the chain, the shape of the weights attached to the chain, and the techniques used.

The *manrikigusari* is also sometimes referred to as *kusari-bundo*, *ryo-bundo*, *sode-kusari*, *kusari*, *tama-kusari*, and *kusari-jutte*.

Samurai who once carried the *manrikigusari* are said to have afforded it with as much respect and care as their sword. The *manrikigusari* was carried by the samurai in many ways. But, when not being carried or in use, it was placed by the samurai on a small plate beside his most frequent sitting place, so that it would be near at hand. When the samurai left home, he usually carried it in his sash.

Special Characteristics of the *Manrikigusari*

General Features

THE MANRIKIGUSARI as it was originally designed by Masaki is said to have had the following characteristics: an iron chain varying in length from one to three feet. At each end of the chain there were small iron weights attached (Fig. 3). These weights were usually of rectangular shape and about two inches long. Although the length of the chain varied, the average length of the *manrikigusari* was about two feet long. Weights of other sizes and shapes were also known to have been used, such as round, octagonal, hexagonal, etc., and were usually employed by other *ryu* (Fig. 4).

The *manrikigusari* is a weapon of defense. It was, and still is, considered one of the most powerful protective weapons among those interesting instruments which are very useful even in contemporary society. It is a perfect weapon for self-defense because of its small size. Truly, if used properly the *manrikigusari* contains the "power and ingenuity of 10,000 persons." It can be used against an attacker's fists or feet, against an opponent armed with a knife, pistol, stick, or sword. The probability of winning under such circumstances is greatly enhanced with the use of the *manrikigusari*.

Advantages to Using the *Manrikigusari*

There is no disadvantage to using the *manrikigusari* in a small room, on a narrow street, along a passageway, or in a public conveyance. In fact, there are many advantages to it. In addition, any one who has knowledge of judo, jujutsu, aikido, karate, or kendo techniques can use the *manrikigusari* as an additional instrument or technique, thereby increasing their effectiveness at self-defense.

As in any other forms of the martial arts, the application of *manrikigusari* techniques must not be offensive—but rather defensive only. When used during a defensive act it must include the action of the entire body and spirit blended as a unit for perfect effectiveness and success. The *manrikigusari* is to be thought of as a living thing; it should not be considered as a dead object. As a weapon, it must be "raised" (reared or nurtured) with you. You and the chain must grow together and become one. If the techniques of the *manrikigusari* are to be mastered, then it must be treated with the highest respect. Should its owner consider it only as a cold piece of weighted chain he will never realize its fullest potential.

Practice

Many painstaking hours must be taken for diligent study and practice. Otherwise there will be no great effectiveness achieved in actual fighting. To fully understand the true secrets of *Masaki-ryu* and the *manrikigusari*, it should be with you at all times. It should be handled like a toy or plaything so that its owner becomes thoroughly familiar with its weight and feel, its length and, of course, its "sting."

The true secret of learning to use the *manrikigusari* and its effectiveness is *SPEED*. It must be used very fast in

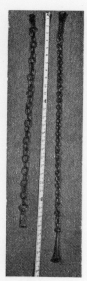

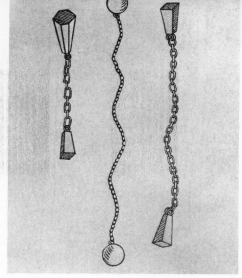

4. Different types of *manrikigusari*

3. Examples of several authentic *manrikigusari*

order to confuse the opponent's ability to distinguish it as a weapon and especially that he should not be able to determine the length of the chain. Slow and sloppy manipulation of the *manrikigusari* can result in catastrophe. It will enable the opponent to seize the chain and possibly disarm the user. The opponent should be struck with lightning fast speed. The *manrikigusari* should then be concealed in another position.

Surprise is another important factor. Strike in one position, then quickly change to another position. Once the *manrikigusari* is used to attack or counter, make every effort to conceal it. Lightning quick action and secrecy are keys to its successful use. To master the use of the *manrikigusari*, the following words best explain its SECRETS:

S peed
E fficiency
C oncealment
R esourcefulness
E nergy
T iming
S urprise

Unique Features

There are various *kyusho* (vital points of the human body) which may be struck with the *manrikigusari*. These are discussed in detail on pages 77–83. Due to its small size the *manrikigusari* is easily carried and concealed anywhere on the person. It may be used to encircle an opponent like a rope and pull him to the ground, to restrain his actions, or to dislodge a weapon from his hands. The chain may be used as a means of blocking against a blow from a sword, knife, or stick when held in the right position. If an opponent attempts to engage you at close quarters, the *manrikigusari* can be shortened or doubled, putting two iron weights into use for striking at random. It may also be used to defend against vicious animals as a form of self-protection.

The *manrikigusari* also has many "non-violent" uses. It may be used to pull a drowning person from the water, or a distressed person from a manhole, a sidewalk or street cave-in, or to rescue someone from a burning building. The various uses to which the *manrikigusari* may be applied are limited only by the ingenuity of the person using it.

Techniques for Using
the *Manrikigusari*

Proper Grip

LEARNING to hold the *manrikigusari* properly is the first step toward successful use. One of the weighted ends is placed in the hand and locked firmly in place with the middle, ring, and little fingers (Fig. 5). The chain is then gathered (but should not be knotted or tangled) and placed on top and locked in place by the thumb. The remaining weight is held in place by the index finger (Fig. 6). Figures 7 and 8 illustrate how the weights are held for attacking vital points of the body.

Manipulation

In executing movements where the *manrikigusari* must swing in circles or semi-circles, it is important that this movement be made through the use of the wrist and not the arm. Since speed is essential, arm movements cause delay and slow the motion of the *manrikigusari* down considerably. Body movements are difficult to explain. To elaborate on them in great detail cannot be done here. The *Iai* techniques make use of moving around from left to right and striking with the *manrikigusari*, kicking or striking horizontally or vertically from upper and lower sides so that the attack is unexpected. Surprise is necessary for effectiveness.

All techniques described herein may be applied with either the right or left hand depending on preference. Please note that all forms and techniques illustrated are performed with a two-foot *manrikigusari* since it is best suited for the techniques of the *Masaki-Ryu*.

Kamae (**Preparatory Positions**)

The foundation of good self-defense is largely dependent upon strong and flexible *kamae* (or preparatory stances). As in other martial arts, the *Masaki-ryu* teaches basic stances or positions that may be assumed in varying situations. Each is designed for a particular purpose and all are flexible enough so that they may be used in combination.

There are five basic *kamae*. They are a direct and important part of the *Masaki-ryu* and are natural enough to enable the individual to perform offensive or defensive maneuvers from any position. They are:

1. *Goho-no-kamae*
2. *Issei-no-kamae*
3. *Tenchi-no-kamae*
4. *Shumoku-no-kamae*
5. *Ippu-no-kamae*

1. *Goho-no-kamae*. To assume this position, stand erect, feet spread apart the approximate width of the shoulders, and distribute the body weight evenly on both feet. This basic standing position of the body and feet is the same in all five positions. The only change will be the position of the hands and the manner in which the *manrikigusari* is held. The *manrikigusari* should be held in the right hand as shown in Figure 6. Cover the right hand with the left to conceal the *manrikigusari* and hold both hands in front of the body as is illustrated in Figures 9 and

10. The *goho-no-kamae* is the foundation for changing to or from all other positions.

5. Initial grip of the *manriki-gusari*

6. The proper complete grip of the *manrikigusari*

7. Grip for attacking the eyes

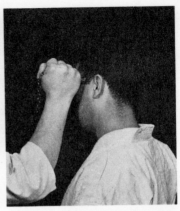

8. Method of attacking the temple

9. *Goho-no-kamae* (front view)

10. *Goho-no-kamae* (side view)

38 SPIKE AND CHAIN

11. *Issei-no-kamae* (front view)

12. *Issei-no-kamae* (side view)

2. *Issei-no-kamae.* Assume the same standing position as for *goho-no-kamae.* Both hands hang naturally to the side of the body. The *manrikigusari* is hidden in the right hand while the left is empty. (One variation is to hold one of the weighted ends in the right hand with the chain hanging naturally along the side of the right leg as shown in Figures 11 and 12.) *Issei-no-kamae* is an excellent position for effective fighting.

14. *Tenchi-no-kamae* (side view)

3. *Tenchi-no-kamae.* In this position, one end of the *manrikigusari* is held in the right hand and the other end in the left hand. The left hand hangs naturally along the left side of the body. The right hand is held at the left shoulder with the chain held taut between both hands. The right arm is held in front of the chest with the right elbow pointing directly forward (Figs. 13 and 14).

16. *Shumoku-no-kamae* (side view)

15. *Shumoku-no-kamae* (front view)

4. *Shumoku-no-kamae*. In this position, the *manriki-gusari* is held with both hands as in *tenchi-no-kamae* except that the left arm is extended at a 45-degree angle to the left rear at shoulder height. The right hand is held in front of the left shoulder with the right elbow pointing straight forward (Figs. 15 and 16).

17. *Ippu-no-kamae* (front view) 18. *Ippu-no-kamae* (rear view)

5. *Ippu-no-kamae.* In this position one end of the *man-rikigusari* is held in the right hand and the other end in the left hand. The chain is held so that it runs diagonally across the back and is held taut. The right hand is positioned just above the right shoulder and the left hand is at waist level (Figs. 17 and 18).

The *Masaki-ryu* has many different forms. The names of the forms that follow are listed in Japanese—their English equivalent is offered as a description only and not as an exact translation since many of these names may be interpreted as having double connotations. Others have non-translatable names and are offered in their original (Japanese) form.

Iai Techniques

1. *Kasumi* (hazing). This technique is performed from the preparatory positions of *goho-no-kamae* or *issei-no-kamae* (Figs. 19 and 20). With the *manrikigusari* concealed in the right hand, step forward with the right foot and throw the *manrikigusari* straight forward extending the right arm in a snapping movement to the front. The action is performed as though you are thrusting with a short knife. (Be sure to hold on to the end of the *manrikigusari* with the right hand so it may be retrieved to another position.) The object is to strike the opponent in the eyes and face with the weighted end of the chain. As this movement is executed, utter a "*kiai.*" *Kiai* is a Japanese word which literally means to "shout" or "scream." In Japan there was once (believed to be still practiced although little known) an art called *kiai-jutsu*, the art of mesmerism through verbal and spiritual projection. To be properly interpreted the *kiai* has generally three important phases or purposes when uttered in performance of a physical action: 1) to add strength to one's technique through proper breathing. Take in a breath through the nostrils and pull it straight down into the lower abdominal region. Exhale about one half of the breath through the mouth and utter the sound *hai* or *aii* retaining almost all the remaining half by pushing down on the lower abdominal region, 2) to psychologically put the opponent in a state of fear or surprise, and 3) to display a strong attitude or spirit.

When executing the *kasumi* technique, the weighted end of the chain is held firmly in the right hand. After striking out at the opponent's face, the arm is bent at the elbow with the palm facing upward so that the chain can be pulled in rapidly or reburied in the fist so that the opponent may be attacked or countered with another technique from a different angle.

19. *Goho-no-kamae*

20. *Issei-no-kamae*

When being attacked by an opponent who approaches from your right side (90 degrees), turn and take a step to your right to face the opponent (Fig. 21). Should he attack from your left side, turn to your left to face him pivoting on your left foot and stepping into him with the right foot (Fig. 22). If the opponent attacks from the rear, pivot on the right foot, bend slightly at the knees to reduce your height and perform the *kasumi* technique as described above (Fig. 23).

When executing the *kasumi* technique from *issei-no-kamae*, the same procedure is followed as above except in this position the *manrikigusari* is thrown from a short point. The opponent will not be able to see it and it will be very difficult to avoid. *The manrikigusari should never be thrown overhand like a baseball or underhand like a bowling ball.*

21. *Kasumi* against approach from the right

22. *Kasumi* against approach from the left

23. *Kasumi* against approach from the rear

24. *Kakoiuchi*

25. *Tenchi-no-kamae*

26. *Shumoku-no-kamae*

27. *Ippu-no-kamae*

2. *Kakoiuchi* (vertical downward strike—vertical "figure 8"). Before this technique is explained the substance of the spiritual attitude behind the *manrikigusari* technique must be thoroughly understood. Such a spiritual attitude must be unified with physical action. This is very important. In order to utilize the full strength of your arm, extend it as much as possible. In using this technique, make a vertical "lasso" motion with the *manrikigusari* before striking (Fig. 24). Determine the point which you wish to strike and then attack with full force. There is a famous Japanese saying that frenzied blows and brute force are ineffective. The secret of the *manrikigusari* techniques is this unity of spiritual and physical action so that flexibility and calmness are achieved. Quick effective motion is the result. The *kakoi-uchi* technique may be executed from *tenchi-no-kamae*, *shumoku-no-kamae*, or *ippu-no-kamae*(Figs. 25, 26, and 27).

From the position of *tenchi-no-kamae* take a step forward with the right foot placing your weight on it. Extend the right hand outward to the front raising the left hand and allowing it to rest on the left hip in striking position (Figs. 28 and 29). Release the weighted end of the *manrikigusari* held in the left hand and with the right hand swing the chain in an overhand arc so that it strikes the opponent's face in a downward circular motion. Allow the chain to travel downward and to your right side. By turning your wrist the chain can be caused to make another arc to strike the opponent with a downward circular motion from the right side, or the chain may be grabbed in the center with the left hand and speedily returned to the *tenchi-no-kamae* position to strike again. Note that this movement is executed as one continuous movement and the chain will in effect have made a vertical "figure 8." This may also be used to stand off an opponent in front of you, by manipulating the *manrikigusari* very "fast"(Fig. 30).

28. Striking position for *kakoi-uchi* (front)

29. Striking position for *kakoi-uchi* (side)

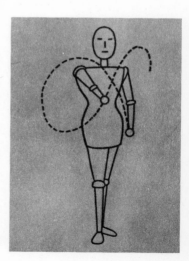

30. Vertical "figure 8"

3. *Sukuiuchi* (upward scooping strike—horizontal "figure 8"). In real fighting situations, effective attack techniques will change from *issei*, *shumoku*, and *ippu-no-kamae*(Figs. 31, 32, and 33). From the *issei-no-kamae* position hold one end of the *manrikigusari* in the right hand and allow the chain to hang naturally along the right leg. Swing the chain upward in a scooping motion to strike the opponent's chin. Continue to swing the *manrikigusari* in a large vertical and circular arc on the right side of your body to strike the opponent again or by manipulating the wrist to the left at the height of the arc, you may make the horizontal "figure 8."

The chain may then be returned to the *tenchi-no-kamae* position by grabbing the center of the chain and pulling it in or it may be gathered up and returned to the *goho-no-kamae* position. When the *sukuiuchi* technique is performed in the horizontal "figure 8" form, it is very useful

31. *Issei-no-kamae*

as a checking technique against opponents standing or approaching from the right and left sides (Fig. 34). (*Note: When performing the kakoiuchi or sukuiuchi techniques it is necessary that the manipulation of the manrikigusari be executed by rotating the wrist and not the arm.*)

32. *Shumoku-no-kamae*

33. *Ippu-no-kamae*

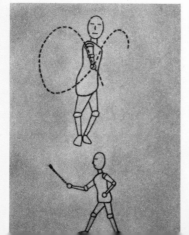

34. Horizontal "figure 8"

35. *Tenchi-no-kamae*

4. *Kobushigarami-nage katame* (fist winding and throwing technique). From the *tenchi-no-kamae* (Fig. 35) position the opponent attacks with a straight punch. Step slightly to the left to avoid it and place the chain under his wrist in the horizontal position and holding it very taut (Fig. 36). With your left hand loop or wind the chain around his wrist (Fig. 37), pull strongly to the side and force him to the ground (Fig. 38). Unwind the chain with the left hand and strike him with *kakoiuchi*, holding the *manrikigusari* in the right hand (Fig. 39). As an alternative to the above you may wind the chain around the opponent's wrist with the left hand and slide the end of the chain held in the right hand slightly up his arm and at the same time push down hard with the left hand to force his arm behind his back to effect a "hammerlock" (Fig. 40). If he continues to resist, kick him in the coccyx (tailbone) with your left knee to bend his back (Fig. 41). Place your left leg behind his legs to trip him to the ground (Figs. 42 and 43). Unwind the chain with the left hand and strike him with *kakoiuchi* with the right hand (Fig. 44). If he punches with the left hand the procedure is reversed.

36. *Kobushigarami* (placing the chain in horizontal position under opponent's wrist)

37. Winding the chain around the wrist

38. Pulling the opponent to the the ground

39. Striking the fallen opponent with *kakoiuchi*

40. Forearm lock

41. Kicking the tailbone with the knee

42. Placing the leg behind the opponent

43. Pushing the opponent to the ground

44. Striking the fallen opponent with *kakoiuchi* with the right hand

45. *Tenchi-no-kamae*

46. *Shumoku-no-kamae*

5. *Udegatame-nage-katame* (forearm lock and throwing technique). From the positions of *tenchi* or *shumoku-no-kamae* (Figs. 45 and 46) avoid the opponent's punch, push, or knife thrust by stepping to the right and placing the chain under his wrist as in *kobushigarami*. Wrap or wind the chain around his wrist with the right hand. Move in closer and push upward with the right hand and pull down hard with the left hand to bend his arm and elbow at a 45-degree angle upward (Fig. 47). With the left hand strike him in the fifth and sixth ribs with the weighted end of the *manrikigusari* extending from the left hand (Fig. 48). If he continues to resist, place your right leg to the rear of his right leg and push him to the ground (Figs. 49 and 50). When he is down strike him by unwinding the chain with the right hand and strike *kakoiuchi* with the left hand (Fig. 51).

47. Locking the arm in *ude-gatame*

48. Striking the opponent's ribs with the left hand

49. Placing the leg behind the opponent

50. Throwing the opponent to the ground

51. Striking the opponent with *kakoiuchi* with the left hand

52. *Tenchi-no-kamae*

53. *Shumoku-no-kamae*

6. *Jodan-uke* (upper block). From the positions of *tenchi* or *shumoku-no-kamae* (Figs. 52 and 53) the opponent attacks with an overhead blow with his hand, stick, or sword (Fig. 54). Hold both ends of the *manrikigusari* and jump in toward the opponent to stop his motion. Hold the chain taut at a diagonal angle (Fig. 55). When this is accomplished, strike the opponent in the eyes with the weighted ends (Fig. 56). Place your forward leg behind him and throw him to the ground. Follow through by striking him with *kakoiuchi*.

54. Defensive position for defense against overhead blow

55. Defending with *jodan-uke*

56. Striking the opponent's eyes

57. Avoiding the opponent's punch in *uchiotoshi*

58. Throwing the chain around the opponent's wrist

7. *Uchiotoshi* (striking drop). From any of the *kamae* positions, avoid the opponent's attack by stepping to the left (Fig. 57). With the right hand swing the *manrikigusari* in an overhand (or backhand) motion and allow it to wrap or wind itself around his arm or weapon (Fig. 58). When it is firmly wound, pull strongly to the side and throw him (Fig. 59) or pull the weapon out of his hands. Follow through by unwinding the chain and striking him with *kakoiuchi*.

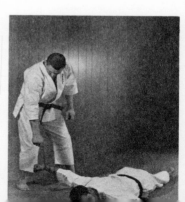

59. Pulling the opponent to the ground

60. *Tenchi-no-kamae*

8. *Shohatsu* (horizontal strike). From the *tenchi* or *shumoku-no-kamae* positions (Figs. 60 and 61) strike out with the chain held in the right hand at horizontal waist level as though you were cutting him in half with a sword at the stomach (Fig. 62). If he avoided the strike by stepping back, take a step forward and strike him on the return swing (Fig. 63). This is the same movement as cutting an enemy with a sword and then sheathing it in the same action. In practicing this movement slash out with the chain as though drawing a sword and in the same action reverse the course of the chain with the wrist to the original position by grabbing it in the center as though returning the sword to the sheath or scabbard. It is important that while performing this movement that the chain remain taut. It should not be allowed to be loose or wavy during this maneuver—speed is very essential.

61. *Shumoku-no-kamae*

62. Striking out with *shohatsu*

63. Striking the opponent with *shohatsu*

64. *Goho-no-kamae*   65. *Tenchi-no-kamae*   66. *Shumoku-no-kamae*

9. *Ukenagashi* (flowing block). From the *goho, tenchi,* or *shumoku-no-kamae* positions (Figs. 64, 65, and 66) hold the *manrikigusari* in front with both hands in the horizontal position with the chain loose or slack between both hands (Fig. 67). When the opponent attacks by pushing, punching, or striking with a stick or sword, tighten the chain with a strong motion at a diagonal angle against his arm or weapon to ward off the attack (Fig. 68). When the opponent attacks with right-handed techniques, step to the right. When he attacks with left-handed techniques, step to the left. The attack should be warded off to one side, taking advantage of the opponent's follow-through. His arm or weapon will slide off the chain. Follow up by striking him in the eyes with the weighted ends extending from both hands (Fig. 69).

67. Holding the chain slack

68. Blocking diagonally with *ukenagashi*

69. Striking the opponent's eyes

70. *Goho-no-kamae*

71. *Tenchi-no-kamae*

72. *Shumoku-no-kamae*

10. *Makiotoshi* (winding drop). From *goho*, *tenchi*, or *shumoku-no-kamae* (Figs. 70, 71, and 72) this technique is used for close fighting by looping the chain around the opponent's neck and throwing him to the ground or may be used for strangling him (Fig. 73). Hold the chain slack as in Figure 67 and make a loop or hoop toward your body. This same technique is used to "lasso" an opponent's arm or weapon. If the technique is used around the opponent's neck he may be struck in the eyes or other vital points. If he is thrown with this technique, unwind the chain and strike him with *kakoiuchi* (see Fig. 51).

73. Looping the chain around the opponent's neck in *maki-otoshi*

74. Carrying the *manriki-gusari* on the belt

75. Drawing the *manrikigusari* from the belt

11. *Yukichigai* (draw and strike). This technique is executed when the *manrikigusari* is carried on the belt (Fig. 74). When practicing this technique or while carrying the *manrikigusari* in this way, care should be taken that the weighted ends do not become tangled in the belt. With the *manrikigusari* looped over the belt, grasp one of the weighted ends with your right hand (Fig. 75). With one fluid motion draw the *manrikigusari* from the belt and swing it diagonally upward in *sukuiuchi* to strike the opponent's chin (Fig. 76). Allow your movement and that of the chain to work together. Once the strike is completed, grab the center of the chain with the left hand. Double the *manrikigusari*, move around to the opponent's rear or side and strike him across the back with both of the weighted ends of the chain (Fig. 77).

76. Striking the opponent's chin with *sukuiuchi*

77. Striking the opponent across the back with doubled chain

78. *Goho-no-kamae*   79. *Issei-no-kamae*

12. *Nageuchi* (throwing strike). There are two forms of *nageuchi*—*ichidan* and *nidan*. *Nageuchi ichidan* (No. 1) is performed by concealing the *manrikigusari* in the fist in the *goho* or *issei-no-kamae* positions (Figs. 78 and 79). The entire *manrikigusari* is thrown into the opponent's face (Fig. 80). It is particularly important that the chain does not scatter in the air. Although this technique may appear to be easy to execute, it takes much hard practice to complete it successfully. The *manrikigusari* should be thrown at a slightly upward angle to overcome its weight. For some, this technique may not seem practical, especially since throwing the *manrikigusari* puts it out of one's use. However, it is one of the formal techniques of the *Masaki-ryu*.

The *nageuchi nidan* (No. 2) technique may be executed from the *issei* or *shumoku-no-kamae* positions when the opponent is running away. If the opponent should run, while chasing him, throw the *manrikigusari* and allow it to wind around one of his legs, then pull him to the ground (Figs. 81 and 82).

80. *Nageuchi ichidan*

81. *Nageuchi nidan*

82. Throwing the chain around the fleeing opponent's ankle

83. *Yokonagare*

84. *Samidare-no-uchi*

Tachiai Techniques

1. *Yokonagare* (checking). This is a technique designed to check the opponent from approaching too closely. Hold the *manrikigusari* in front of the body horizontally with the chain taut. The opponent will be restrained from coming closer. This technique may also be used in conjunction with other techniques when the situation warrants (Fig. 83).

2. *Samidare-no-uchi* (body shifting, horizontal striking, and kicking). Double the *manrikigusari* and while holding both ends in either the right or left hand, strike the opponent while moving forward or backward and kicking him simultaneously (horizontal strike shown in Fig. 84).

86. *Yadome*

85. *Kagero-no-uchi*

3. *Kagero-no-uchi* (body shifting, vertical upward strike, and kick). Hold the *manrikigusari* in either the right or left hand while making forward or backward body movements. Strike the opponent with *sukuiuchi* and at the same time kick him in the vital points (Fig. 85).

4. *Yadome* (arrow stop or shield technique). Step forward with the right foot and shift the body weight forward. Hold one end of the *manrikigusari* in the right hand and extend the right arm forward. Swing the *manrikigusari* in front of the body as if to form a shield (Fig. 86). Do not move the arm while executing this movement. Turn the *manrikigusari* with the wrist only. This technique is called *yadome* (arrow stop) because its purpose is to make a shield in front of the body (as if to stop an arrow). This is an excellent checking technique to prevent an opponent's advance.

Henka (Variations)

1. *Kobushi kujiki* (fist crushing). This is a versatile technique that may be applied in a variety of situations. While holding the weighted ends of the *manrikigusari*, a small portion of the weight is allowed to extend or protrude beyond the hand so that it may be used to strike an attacking opponent's fist. It may also be applied to defenses against choking, lapel seizure, pushing, etc., by striking the opponent's arm, wrist, hand, or other vital points (Fig. 87).

2. *Suneori* (shin striking). This technique is applied in the same manner as *kobushi kujiki*, except that it is used to attack the opponent's shins (Fig. 88).

87. *Kobushi kujiki*

88. *Suneori*

89. One hand chain seizure

Other Variations

Although the following techniques are not part of the true *Masaki-ryu*, they are examples that illustrate that there is literally no end to the number of combinations that may be executed with the *manrikigusari*.

1. Defense against chain seizure (one hand). Should the opponent seize one end of the chain with one hand (or both) through carelessness or improper handling, with your free hand (the one that is not holding the *manrikigusari*) grasp the center of the chain and release the end that is being held by you by swinging it toward your opponent's face. As the opponent is struck, pull hard to release the *manrikigusari* from his hand and strike him again if necessary with another technique (Fig. 89). Another alternative is to quickly wrap the chain around the opponent's wrist and pull him to the ground.

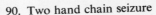
90. Two hand chain seizure

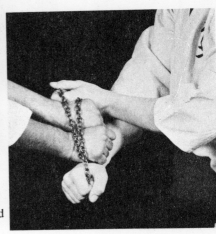

91. Winding the chain around the opponent's wrists

2. Defense against chain seizure (two hands). Should the opponent seize the center of the chain with both hands (Fig. 90) quickly wind the chain around both of his wrists and pull strongly to cause his submission (Fig. 91) or, after you have wound the chain around his wrists raise his arms slightly (Fig. 92), pivot around and place your left shoulder under his elbows (Fig. 93), raise up with your shoulder and pull down strongly with both hands. Should this prove ineffective pull the opponent forward, lift with both legs (Fig. 94), pull strongly with both hands and throw him over your shoulder to the ground (Fig. 95). Follow through by keeping his wrists tied together and stamping him in the throat, face, or other vital points with your foot.

92. Raising the opponent's arms

93. Inserting the left shoulder under the opponent's elbows

94. Pulling the opponent forward and lifting with the legs

95. Throwing the opponent over the shoulder and to the ground

96. Winding the chain around the opponent's ankle in defense of a kick

97. Countering the opponent's kick with a kick to the vital points

3. Defense against kicking. Avoid the opponent's kick by stepping to one side and winding the chain around his ankle (Fig. 96). Counter by kicking the opponent in the testicles (Fig. 97); or, avoid the opponent's kick, swing the chain under his ankle—(horizontally Fig. 98)—step forward, lift his leg as high as possible to throw him to the ground (Fig. 99); or, avoid the opponent's kick, wrap the chain around his ankle, step inside of the kicking leg, hook your leg around his supporting leg (Fig. 100), pull his leg out strongly to throw him (Fig. 101). Follow through by kicking him in the vital points.

98. Catching the opponent's leg in defense of a kick

99. Raising the opponent's leg to throw him to the ground

100. Hooking the opponent's leg

101. Throwing the opponent by reaping his leg

Kyusho

KYUSHO (vital points of the human body) are areas of the body that are susceptible to the application of force or pressure, the result of which will bring pain, unconsciousness, or death. The degree of force or pressure applied can cause one, two, or all three phases. The area of the body to which the force or pressure is applied are also necessary considerations. Striking or attacking some areas will cause only pain, others may result in the person's loss of consciousness, and if excessive force is used, death will be the result. Therefore, the amount of force, the means by which the force is applied, and the area of the body that is attacked should always be seriously contemplated.

Through fast manipulation, the *manrikigusari* is capable of producing a tremendous force. It should never be directed at a vital point of the body in jest or playfulness. It is not difficult to damage an eye or lose several teeth during practice by oneself, notwithstanding the bruises that may be incurred through careless handling. In studying this chapter, be constantly mindful that the attack and counterattack with the *manrikigusari* against the vital points of the human body are designed to seriously disable or to kill.

1. *Tendo* (crown of the head): This area may be attacked by doubling the *manrikigusari* and striking the opponent with both of the weighted ends at the same time, by *kakoiuchi* or with the *kobushi kujiki* technique.

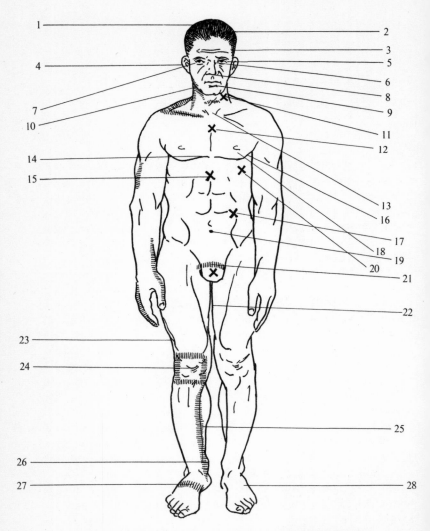

102. *Kyusho*—vital points of the human body (front)

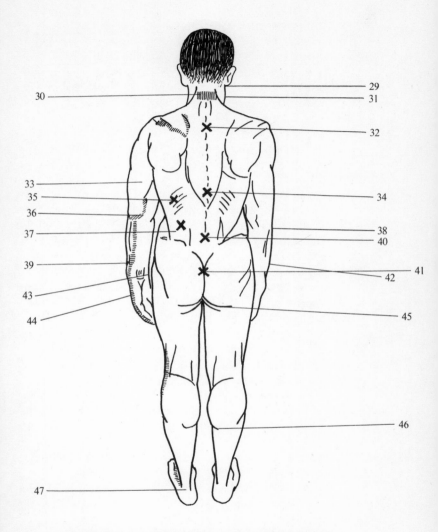

103. *Kyusho*—vital points of the human body (rear)

2. *Tento* (the fontanelle or space between the crown of the head and the forehead): Highly vulnerable to lethal attack with *kakoiuchi* or the *kobushi kujiki* technique.

3. *Komekami* (the temple): Also a very susceptible vital spot which can be effectively attacked with *kakoiuchi*, *shohatsu*, or the *kobushi kujiki* technique.

4. *Mimi* (the ears): Methods of attack are the same as for numbers 1, 2, and 3.

5. *Seidon* (area above and below the eyes): Vulnerable to attack by *kasumi*, *kakoiuchi*, and the *kobushi kujiki* techniques.

6. *Miken* (nasion or summit of the nose in the center of the forehead): Area midway between the eyes can be fatally attacked with *kasumi*, *kakoiuchi*, or the *kobushi kujiki* technique.

7. *Gansei* (eyeballs): Attack with *kasumi*, *nage-uchi* *kakoiuchi*, or *kobushi kujiki* technique.

8. *Jinchu* (the philtrum or spot just under the nose): Death can be caused by a strong blow with the *kobushi kujiki* technique or with *sukuiuchi*.

9. *Gekon* (spot beneath the lower lip): Highly vulnerable to the *kobushi kujiki* technique, *kasumi*, or *kakoiuchi*.

10. *Mikazuki* (the jaw): Attack with *sukuiuchi*, *kobushi kujiki*, *shohatsu*, or the doubled chain.

11. *Hichu* (base of the throat, Adam's apple or projection of the thyroid cartillage of the larynx): Vulnerable to lethal blows with the *kobushi kujiki*, *kasumi*, *sukuiuchi*, or doubled chain.

12. *Danchu* (summit of the breastbone or sternum): Attack with *kobushi kujiki*.

13. *Sonu* (spot between the throat and top of the breastbone or sternum): Methods of attack are *kobushi kujiki*, doubled chain, or *shohatsu*.

14. *Kyototsu* (the base of the breastbone or sternum):

Attack with *kobushi kujiki*, doubled chain, or *shohatsu*.

15. *Suigetsu* (the solar-plexus): Attack with *kobushi kujiki*, or *shohatsu*.

16. *Kyoei* (below the armpits, approximately between the fifth and sixth ribs): Attack with *kobushi kujiki* or *shohatsu*.

17. *Inazuma* (side of the body slightly above the hips): Attack with *kobushi kujiki* or *shohatsu*.

18. *Ganchu* (spot below the nipples): Attack with *kobushi kujiki* or *shohatsu*.

19. *Myojo* (spot about an inch below the navel): Attack with *kobushi kujiki* or *shohatsu*.

20. *Denko* (spot between the seventh and eighth ribs): Attack with *kobushi kujiki* technique or *shohatsu*.

21. *Kinteki* (testicles): Attack with *kobushi kujiki* or *sukuiuchi*.

22. *Yako* (inside of upper thigh): Vulnerable to attack by *sukuiuchi* or *shohatsu*.

23. *Fukuto* (outside of lower part of thigh): Methods of attack are the same as those for *yako*.

24. *Hizakansetsu* (knee joint): Can be kicked in connection with *sukuiuchi* or struck with *shohatsu*.

25. *Kokotsu* (the center point of the tibia or shinbone): Attack with *suneori* or *shohatsu*.

26. *Uchikurobushi* (inside of the ankle joint): Attack with *kobushi kujiki*, *suneori*, or *shohatsu*.

27. *Kori* (upper surface of the instep): Attack with *shohatsu* or *suneori*.

28. *Kusagakure* (top outer edge of the foot): Methods of attack are *suneori* or *shohatsu*.

29. *Dokko* (the mastoid process or spot behind the ears): Attack with the *kobushi kujiki* technique or *shohatsu*.

30. *Keichu* (nape of the neck): Attack with the *kobushi kujiki* technique, *shohatsu*, or doubled chain.

31. *Shofu* (side of the neck): Attack with the *kobushi*

kujiki technique or *shohatsu*.

32. *Soda* (spot between the shoulder blades): Attack with the *kobushi kujiki* technique or doubled chain.

33. *Wanshun* (back of arm, top of outside edge of upper arm): Attack with the *kobushi kujiki* technique or *shohatsu*.

34. *Katsusatsu* (spot below *soda*): Attack with same methods as 32.

35. *Jinzo* (kidney): Methods of attack are the same as 32.

36. *Hijizume* (elbow joint): Attack with *udegatame* or *shohatsu*.

37. *Kanzo* (liver): Methods of attack are the same as for those of 32.

38. *Udekansetsu* (arm joint): Methods of attack are the same as for 36.

39. *Kote* (wrist or back of the lower forearm): Attack with *kakoiuchi*, *ukenagashi*, *kobushi kujiki*, or *kobushigarami*.

40. *Kodenko* (base of the spine): Attack with same methods as for 32 and 34.

41. *Bitei* (the coccyx)—(small triangular bone ending human spinal column): Attack same as 32 or knee or foot by kicking.

42. *Sotojakuzawa* (outer portion of the forearm): Attack with *udegatame* or *shohatsu*.

43. *Uchijakuzawa* or *miyakudokoro* (inner parts of the forearm where pulsation can be felt): Attack with *kobushigarami*.

44. *Shuko* (back of the hand): Attack with *kakoiuchi* or *kobushi kujiki*.

45. *Ushiro-inazuma* (spot below the buttocks): Method of attack are the same as for 32.

46. *Sobi* (spot on inside of the lower part of the leg, at the base of the calf): Attack with *shohatsu* or *nageuchi nidan*.

47. *Akiresuken* (Achilles tenden): Attack same as 46.

(Note: Shaded areas and those marked with "X" are highly vulnerable and most commonly used.)

It is essential that anyone pursuing the knowledge and proficiency of the *manrikigusari*, thoroughly familiarize himself with *kyusho*. Without this knowledge, and if engaged in a serious struggle with an armed opponent, it would be improbable that he could be dealt with efficiently or effectively. The inadvertent striking at any area of the body is leaving too much to chance. Even famous swordsmen of Japan devoted their entire lives to developing a single technique to dispatch one or more adversaries with one slash of their swords. But, this technique could not be effective if it were directed just anywhere at the body.

How to Make a *Manrikigusari*

AN ORIGINAL *manrikigusari* is extremely difficult if not impossible to obtain. On a recent trip to Japan, the author succeeded in finding only two, one very old, the other of more recent vintage. During the past 40 years Mr. Yumio Nawa has found only about 16. The unavailability of the *manrikigusari* leaves only one alternative for those who wish to pursue the practice of *Masaki-ryu*—and that is to undertake the making of one personally.

As mentioned in preceding chapters, the *manrikigusari* ranges in lengths of one, two, and three feet. It may be a good idea to have one of each, since there is not much more trouble in making three, once the materials are obtained, than there is in making only one. The prospective student should bear in mind that the techniques explained in previous chapters of this book are best applied to a *manrikigusari* with a two-foot chain.

Antique (or original) *manrikigusari* were handmade. The chain as well as the weights were forged by hand. To have a good blacksmith make one in this manner would cost a great deal of money. The next best alternative is to seek out modern materials and methods. The *manrikigusari* consists of two main parts, the chain and the weights. It is important (as the user will soon realize once his *manrikigusari* is made and used) that the size and weight of the chain as well as the size, shape, and weight of the weights be in balance. To use a heavy chain and small light weights, or a small light chain with heavy weights will cause the *manrikigusari* to be out of balance. The chain will not respond to your manipulation and will have a tendency to "whip" or "snarl."

The Chain

In selecting a chain it is suggested that the student obtain a Number 3, straight (welded) link machine chain, plated or unplated. This may be obtained at most hardware stores for a few cents a foot. Heavy chain, locked-link chain, dog-leash chain, etc., are not desirable. It is difficult to manipulate these types of chain and some varieties are not strong enough to withstand rugged use. To use an inferior type of chain may endanger your safety as well as that of others. The type and size chain recommended above is the only type that conforms to the size and weight of the original types of *manrikigusari*.

The Weights

The types of weights that were attached to original *manrikigusari* were made of steel, iron, or brass. You will find, however, that obtaining suitable weights for your *manrikigusari* will be much more difficult than the chain. They may be hand forged by a blacksmith or the student may go to a pattern maker and have one duplicated in wood. This pattern (although expensive) may then be taken to a foundry and as many of the weights may be cast as may be desired. In selecting a suitable weight, the size, shape, and weight should conform to the following:

1. The weight should be made of steel, iron, or brass. Lighter metals such as aluminum are too light.

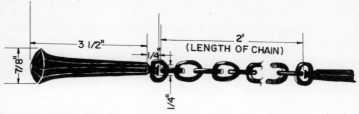

104. Specifications for making a *manrikigusari*

2. The size (width and length) should be large enough to hold in the hand to execute some of the necessary techniques for striking.

3. The weight should not be too heavy nor should it be too light. It must balance with the size and weight of the chain.

When a suitable chain and weights have been selected, the student is then faced with the problem of fastening or attaching the weights to the chain. You will find that an experienced welder will be very helpful in solving this problem. The last link of the chain may be cut (or sawed) open and attached to the weights. The welder can then braze over the opening to close it. Be certain that the opening is well closed and that the weight will not break loose during use. You are then prepared to pursue some very interesting practice. Figure 104 is a detailed drawing of a *manrikigusari* in the author's possession. It's dimensions are exact and is offered as a guide to anyone who wishes to make one of his own.

PART II
THE SECRETS OF
SHURIKEN-JUTSU

105. Samurai throwing the *shaken*

History of *Shuriken-jutsu*

The art of *shuriken-jutsu* dates back to the Edo period (about 150 years ago). At that time, a samurai in Miyagi Prefecture was known to have mastered the techniques of concealing five *shuriken* (needles) and when the occasion presented itself would pull them one at a time with his fingers and throw them at his enemy.

During ancient times in Japan, women were known to carry certain weapons or implements for self-protection. Among them were the *kaiken* (short knife) and the *kanzashi* (a form of ornamental hairpin). When prominent women, or those serving at palaces were attacked by intruders or bandits, they used the *kaiken* or needles for self-defense. The knives or needles were usually about four inches long and at a short distance, they could be thrown like *shuriken*. These implements were highly regarded because of their small size, particularly since they could be concealed in a small handbag or pocket. The eyes and other vital points of the attacker were usually the targets. Women of less prominence also used the *kanzashi* or ornamental hairpin for the same purposes and with the same deadly results. The *kanzashi* are tipped with a sharp point like that of a knife or sword. The sides are spoon shaped which usually contained some form of poison to insure the attacker's death. Weapons of these shapes can still be seen in Japan today.

The Transition

Shuriken-jutsu (*shuriken*—a pointed missile thrown by hand, *jutsu*—art) is first known to have begun with the use of needle-like missiles made of iron or steel and varying in length from three to ten inches. Later the form changed to the use of the *tanto* (or short sword) and finally reverted back to the needle-like *shuriken* as it is known today. The *tanto* were probably abandoned because they were never primarily designed to be thrown, were expensive, and could not be carried in quantity as could the *shuriken*. At the present time there are only about ten *shuriken* men in Japan. One of them is Mr. Isamu Maeda (judo 5th Dan), who practiced the *shuriken* techniques in China during the war.

Through the years the *shuriken* has changed considerably to various types, sizes, and shapes. In Japan at this time the three most widely known *ryu* (or schools) are: *Negishi-ryu*, *Shirai-ryu*, and *Chisin-ryu*. The Negishi *shuriken* are shaped like narrow torpedoes and are sharpened in a hexogonal shape with a tassel on the end. Their length is about 10 inches. The tassels aid the *shuriken* in its flight to the target. Nothing is known about the other two schools.

Various Types of *Shuriken*

There are about 20 kinds and shapes of *shuriken* (Fig. 106). Some are short and stubby, others are long and thin, still others are round and thick, square, or flat and square. There are those with only one end sharpened and those with both ends sharpened.

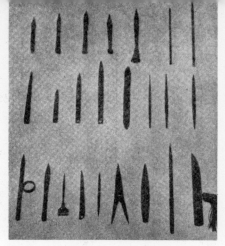

106. Various kinds of *shuriken*

Shuriken which are to be used for self-defense are said to be required to conform to the following: They should be small and easy to carry. When thrown, they should be unnoticed and unavoidable by the enemy. This is one of the reasons why the enemy is usually allowed to come close, so that he may be struck accurately in the eyes or other vital areas.

Proper Method of Holding the *Shuriken*

The *shuriken* is placed in the palm of the hand with all four fingers extended and is held in place with the thumb. It should be held high in the palm with the end touching the tips of the fingers for short distances and low in the palm for long distances (Figs. 107 and 108). The following are a very brief but exacting explanation of the true techniques of *shuriken-jutsu*. If the reader wishes to perfect these techniques with the *shuriken*, he must devote time to diligent practice and endeavor with great patience.

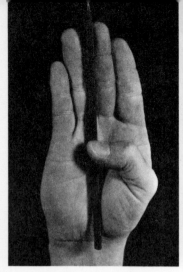 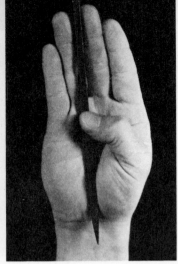

107. Proper method of holding the *shuriken* (point up)

108. Proper method of holding the *shuriken* (point down)

The Secrets of *Shuriken-jutsu*

1. The time, atmosphere, physical condition, the shape and weight of the weapon, and the target must be balanced. The weapon must be thrown quickly and straight into the target. The target will then be struck at right angles.

2. At the instant the weapon is thrown, you should feel as if a bird has slipped out of your hand.

3. If you use all the strength in your hand and shoulder and if you put strength into your hip, the flying weapon will penetrate even a wooden wall.

4. There are various forms of throwing the *shuriken*, but they all depend upon having "emptiness of mind."

5. When throwing at a short distance, bend your body and you will be able to strike faster and with all your strength (Fig. 109).

109. Stance for throwing the *shuriken* at short distances

110. Stance for throwing the *shuriken* at longer distances

6. For longer distances, straighten your body, expand your chest, and take your time to aim and throw (Fig. 110).

7. When you strike at an enemy, your spiritual attitude should be like the flexibility of the bamboo tree heavily laden with snow. When the weight becomes too great the tree bends from the load and snaps back into its original position throwing the snow from its leaves.

8. When making preparation to strike an enemy, your preparations must be unseen. The enemy must suspect nothing from your bearing, movements, or appearance.

9. The secret of striking quickly is in your fingers and your breathing.

10. When preparing to strike at the enemy, your preparations and position should be like the frost settling on the ground on a dark night. It is quiet, with no shape, and yet is all pervasive.

11. Inhale 80% of your breath into the stomach. Then you will have such a reserve of air that you will have no need to breathe while striking.

12. Do not look at the enemy with your physical eyes. You must penetrate the target of him with your spiritual eyes.

13. You should not try to strike the enemy with your physical power. You must combine it with your spiritual strength.

14. When your mind is "empty" your weapon will go straight. When it is clouded, your weapon will go wrong.

15. Your spiritual attitude must also be like the bamboo holding heavy snow. You should be slow but powerful, sure and calculated when you strike the target; never jerky and anxious.

16. If your mind is like the moon's reflection on the water of a pond no threat can alter its basic calm. A moon reappears on the water's surface after a stone ripples it. Your movements should not be sluggish and should not be your sole concern. Do not let your mind interfere with your physical movements but it should be the origin of their fluidity.

Practice

If you practice the physical skills of this art diligently and have the proper spiritual attitude, you will perfect it. A close enemy is still dangerous even if you have confidence in your fighting skills. When there is a distance of several feet between you and your enemy, you may have a chance to defeat him. But, at the critical moment, it is very difficult to strike the enemy at a distance such as two or three feet. This is why the principle of *kanime* is important in the *shuriken* arts. *Kanime* (crab's eye) is that which you should be able to see in your opponent's eyes.

If the enemy's sword tip is only several steps away from your left hand (which is holding the *shuriken* horizontally) and if you make the distinction between the white and black (colors) parts of your enemy's eyes, and it seems as if this black part (or crab's eye) jumps out at you, it is at this black part which you should throw your *shuriken*. If you are holding just one *shuriken*, accuracy will determine your fate. But, if you cannot see the black part of your enemy's eyes, this is the moment your fate will be realized. You will surely be cut down by the enemy's sword. There is no need to throw the weapon into the enemy's face, you merely insert the *shuriken* into the enemy's eyes with both hands and die together.

Half-turn Method

At a short distance, the *shuriken* when thrown will make only a half turn in the air before it strikes the target. At a longer distance, the *shuriken* will make full turns, depending upon the distance thrown. For this distinction, the *shuriken* must be held properly with the end pointing toward the wrist and at the proper height in the palm (as previously discussed).

Target Selection

Finding a suitable target for practice is a very simple matter. Several 2″ × 2″ planks about three or four feet in length and nailed together with a crosspiece in the back make an excellent target. Soft white pine is recommended because it is easy to penetrate. The best source is your

111. An outdoor target for throwing the *shuriken*

local lumber yard or at the site of a dismantled old building. Archery targets, bales of hay, etc., may also be used but they do not allow the *shuriken* to penetrate and "stick" like they should. You may want to paint or spray a "bullseye" on your target. An excellent example of an outdoor target is shown in Figure 111.

Safety Precautions

Although small, the *shuriken* can be very dangerous if improperly used. Extreme care should be taken that spectators stand well out of the way during your throwing practice. *Shuriken* can take some unpredictable bounces. Practice should be conducted outdoors giving much attention to the possibility of error, and damage to private or public property.

Throwing and Distance

Although the methods of holding the *shuriken* and other

important information with regard to throwing have already been discussed, there are several other important factors that will greatly aid the thrower to succeed in throwing accurately. The first is that when throwing, the wrist should be locked and should never be allowed to snap or bend during an actual throw. Failure to keep the wrist in a locked position will cause the *shuriken* to turn excessively in its normal course to the target. The second is the distance to the target. The *shuriken* will naturally turn on its way to the target. The thrower must compute the number of turns according to the distance the *shuriken* is thrown. At short distances (as previously discussed) the *shuriken* will turn only one half turn. At longer distances it will turn one or more full turns. It is suggested that the thrower begin by standing very close (several feet away) and throw the *shuriken* at the target. If it is thrown point up it should go straight into the target without turning. Move back a few feet at a time and each time throw the *shuriken* at the target. When the *shuriken* sticks in the target you have found your distance for one full turn. For the man of average height the *shuriken* should make one full turn in approximately 12 to 15 feet. Use the same procedure for finding your distance for throwing the *shuriken* at one half, or more turns. If you are right handed, stand with the right foot forward, and as you throw, step forward with the left foot (like throwing a ball). (Figs. 109 and 110.)

If the *shuriken* hits flat against the target with the point upward, it will be necessary for you to step backward a step or two. If it hit the target with the point downward, you must step forward a foot or two. If the *shuriken* strikes the target with the unsharpened end or if it strikes sometimes with the point up and sometimes with the point down, then chances are that you may be bending your wrist.

Once you have found your distance, mark the spot or use some method for measuring it. You then have the proper distance for a perfect throw every time. Coordination is very important and is necessary if you hope to stick the target consistently. Accuracy is developed only by regular practice.

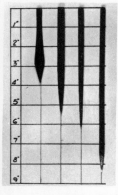

112. Length of some *shuriken* shown in inches

How to Make Your Own *Shuriken*

The *shuriken* are much easier to make and the materials much easier to obtain than for the *manrikigusari*. Any steel company or supply house can provide you with a sufficient quantity of 1/4″ bar stock. The steel can be sawed into desired lengths (6″ and 8-1/4″ are best for throwing) and then put on a grinder and the ends sharpened (or tapered), to a point approximately one inch back from the end. The *shuriken* may be made in as large a quantity as is desired. *Shuriken* men in Japan usually carry five or six at a time. Larger quantities are of course more desirable for practice because it eliminates the constant walking back and forth to the target. (See Fig. 112 for detailed length of some *shuriken*.)

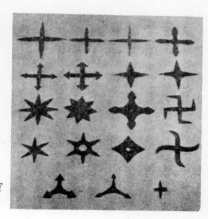

113. Various kinds of *shaken*

Shaken

The *shaken* are cross-shaped *shuriken* with three points, six points, and eight points (Fig. 113). Movies and television in Japan have recently made them popular again. The *shaken* travel through the air in an end-over-end fashion before they find their target. When thrown accurately and at right angles, they are sure to find their target as they have many sharp cutting edges. It is therefore very easy to throw the *shaken* and to strike the target, but, if one desires to accomplish some degree of proficiency, he must practice.

If the *shaken* (or "vehicle knives" as they are sometimes called) are compared with the "needle type" *shuriken*, they can be seen to have some advantages as well as disadvantages. *Shaken* are to some degree inconvenient to carry because of their many sharp and protruding edges. However, distance is not relatively important when throwing the *shaken* as it is when throwing the *shuriken*. If your accuracy is good, there should be no trouble in finding the

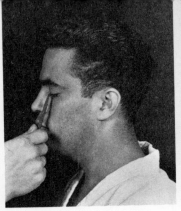

114. Method of attacking the eyes with the *shuriken*

115. Method of attacking the throat with the *shuriken*

opponent's eyes or other vital parts of the body as the *shaken* will stick no matter how they are thrown. As with the *shuriken* (Figs. 114 and 115) the *shaken* can also be used without throwing it. It may be held in the fist so that its points protrude beyond the fingers to attack certain vital points of the body. At close encounters with an opponent, it may be used to strike his fist, legs, or other areas making it a very formidable weapon.

In ancient times, when the *shaken* were used by the samurai, poison or horse dung was put on the points. An enemy struck with this *shaken* would die in fever from the poison or tetanus bacteria. Sometimes, a fuse and explosive compound was put on the weapon and was ignited before thrown, thus exploding when it struck the enemy. The *shaken* were also referred to as "fire-vehicle knives" and could be used for igniting fires from a distance.

Bibliography

Nawa, Yumio: *Jutte Hojo-No Kenkyu* (The Jutte Arresting Rope Study), Yuzankaku Publishing Company, Tokyo, Japan, 1964.

Harry K. McEvoy and Charles V. Gruzanski: *Knife Throwing as a Modern Sport*, Charles C. Thomas, Publisher, Springfield, Illinois, 1965.

Harrison, E. J.: *The Fighting Spirit of Japan*, Unwin, London, 1913.